TREMOR

∞

TREMOR

Poems

Marisol Baca

THREE MILE HARBOR PRESS

New York

Three Mile Harbor Press
PO Box 1
Stuyvesant, New York 12173
www.3mileharborpress.com

ISBN: 978-0-9983406-1-6

Library of Congress Control Number: 2017958500

First Edition
Printed in the United States of America

Book design and author photo by Curtis W. Messer
Cover art by Erin Webster © All Rights Reserved

*This book is dedicated to my parents, Barbara and Mario,
and to my husband, Curtis*

CONTENTS

THE HORNO

Here is my father's body moving
over the frame of the kiln
mud mound, size of a cellar,
after time
it begins to resemble an ant hill.

One September the cupola was built,
a mixture of clay and straw stalks
carried from Grandpa's dark blue
Ford Pickup.
Red heap it looked like, in the distance.

A dark tunnel is dug in the earth
good for smoking freshwater trout
which the men catch
in the rivers and lakes.

The bricks will take days
to settle and dry. I count fox
tails and stomp in the marsh
beside the alfalfa fields.
Mother is on the creamsicle-phone,
she has orders.

The crib is now much too small for me.
Horno in the rain is deep red.
I rub my hand over its surface
and it bleeds
purple like blackberries.

Inside,
with frozen peas in my mouth
I watch dad shaping
the final bricks,
the sun had changed him to a horse,
no undershirt, hair black
and long like Jesus in photos.

Trout in lakes and rivers.
The smoke in wisps along the road,
long trails of feathers beside the fields, lakes, and rivers,
the trout inside the rivers.

Dad buys ducks in the winter.
Mom tells stories to Grandpa,
I follow the ducks into the furnace
and fall asleep. Snow covered,
it becomes a hilly shadow
stretched at noon, gloomy and long.

Clouds, same color as the inside of that thing.

Smoke paints the walls in ash.

Feathers left over and over from the ducks.

They disappeared after months.

I didn't cry when they were gone.

He used to smoke trout in it, my father.

Magdalena, I am praying to you.

I have fallen asleep inside the old horno again.

SARCOPHAGI IN GLASS HOUSES

*After Magdalena Abakanowicz's installation at The
Storm King Art Center & the death of my Great Aunt*

I.

Manuelita sent Mom and Auntie Patsy

into the podding room

piles of chile

skins like dried meat

Mom and Auntie Patsy hitching

the meat out

pulling the seeds and membrane

from the inner lining

little fingers tugging at the green tongues

speechless in their hands

packing them into glass jars

The day of death was passing by

the coffin on the coffee table

the old sitting together

the men's heads

white and scattered

like seeds

Manuelita passing out crocheted kerchiefs

monogrammed and stained

Uncle Benito had to hold on
his wife looked up from the coffee table
she looked up but was already dead
Auntie Patsy was tired
of the piles that smelled burnt
the piles my mom kept jumping in

The look of the chilies
mouthless
stemless
plucked
the candles were lit
the little earthen room

Rain fell with tin sounds on the roof
The dead woman smiled from the trees

They had welts on their hands
The chili had been too hot to eat

II.

 The chiles arrive in pods
The pods are much too tight
They break the sides open

III.

Manuelita constructed her home
with an horno in the kitchen
she only burned cedar wood
she had burn marks along her arms
kept feeding the horno
glass shards
cedar wood
but we sold that house
we sold the great cottonwoods
outside that house
and the red chile *ristras*
those she plumed
and fed to us

IV.

It was in New York,
much later
I walked in the hills
and stayed close to the water
away from the groves
I found these constructed graves
these insect wrappings

these mummies
and all I could do
was talk to her
I think she hoped
I'd come along
take hold of her
move her story
across the weatherworn panes
tell her New York is the secret
passage to Corrales, New Mexico,
near the horses
near the great white sand dunes
near the adobe house
built around her imprint

Hatch chile in August
rain, acidity,
the roasters large as entry rooms, foyers
churning pods by the hundreds
the burn in our lungs
the burn in our eyes
the whole town crying
and the women by the stove
glass houses make for good mirrors

V.

Great Gods of the mountainside
please spare us the duty of eating
please spare us the acid tongue
the skins and their veins burst
and smell of her
the casings by the *molcajete*
like translucent tombs
waiting to lend themselves to stone
waiting to affect the mouth
the acerbic bite and the swelling
waiting, waiting for the opiates
of the body to pump and roll

VI.

Houses the dead
houses the lines
and the lines
between us
houses the slow
shag in our dark past
past the houses on the right
the houses on fire

houses the houses on fire

the houses that house

how houses have past

lined by lines

lines of grass

lined pictures fading on walls

lined windows,

shingles, and rats

and the houses house us,

the dead and us

THE DISCOVERY

They found the nautilus
at the peak of the Sandia Mountains
in a crag, they said.
The sun shone through it.
And all the mysteries of its labyrinth glowed.
It had a story the petrified animals shared with it,
and measure by measure it fed itself on the land,
it suffocated in the slime and dark
dollops of nothingness,
it turned into a moonstone,
and reminded one of the Pueblo Indians of the sea.
He recalled his dreams of the dolphins,
his nightmares of their shrieking and singing,
and his fantasies of the seaweed and its blotted smell.
It had ancient teeth inside its body swirl.

How it had come to the highest peak was an anomaly.
The ocean was nowhere,
except in the recesses of their minds,
like libraries made of pyrite
like paper bridges, and tiny doors opening to nothing.
They were afraid of the gristle
in its living chamber,

they were scared it would understand them

and try to crawl away, or fly.

Much more fantastic than Velociraptor footprints;

it was a residue in their hearts,

a tentacular lust;

sucking them free of the valley they traveled from.

They forgot about their wives at home roasting chili.

They forgot about their son's respectable long limbs,

and fishing under rock formations deep in the woods.

They forgot everything

except that spaceship of deep;

how it ached in them.

And it was angry for trees

underwater,

for purple and green and teal inkiness.

It reminded them of Heron Dam,

and the ammonites they found there,

big as tabletops.

Hundreds of them left over

from some great inland sea.

They said the discovery was old as earth,

they said it had seen the nebulas and the bowl

of space from its foggy eye.

VELELLA VELELLA

It was the sight of death we saw first.
The long silent beach and the warm carcasses of the
jellies—
thousands of them—camped—waiting for the end.

Little cellophane boats entangled in kelp.
The sail-like appendages had the suggestion of sliced ginger.
The clump-float was once buoyant on the water.
Some became nests for sand fleas.

Some lay in a pool of salt and brine.
Their clear sails shivering against the day's breeze.

Some piled,
letting their color leak into the sand below,
a crackle of blue fire and purple ooze.
And some still sailing in the afternoon tide—
humming to themselves,
drifting songs for zooids.

How long did they wander?
Their hollow tentacles were ghost hairs
collecting the floating life beneath.

Slowly they maundered into death, guided by the wind.

My father filled his pockets with them

and walked along the ocean throwing them back.

MEMORY AND DISEASE IN THE TROPICS

Monsoon and darkness from the rivers came upon you,
washed you.
Dream-turn—a jungle of lost bones.
But you were left, at least, with the scent of it.
Banana leaves, rain collected along their great living spines.
They tear and yellow on the edges, darken and dissolve.
Oak leaves—the water oxen score
their hoof-prints across them.
Morning mist and smoke rises just beneath the great oak.
Poplar leaves—the hearts eaten away by fungi spots
Her markings scatter like confetti.

And my grandfather,
My father.
What was there, has left.
The veinlets gone awry
Left these men in a world of margins.
My grandfather looking for substance, is obscured by fog.
My father, quicksand.
He is up to his neck,
breathes in, but can't see solid earth.

A hurried note, these stories:

The small glow in the dripping water.

A slimy stagnant pond.

The bough reaching its limit.

Lichen, overgrowth, fern-layered
cupola.

MEMORY OF THE CARD GAME

He knows his five-card draw.

It's the only thing that takes his mind off panic.

Panic is that my mom is with Grandma at the hospital,

and he forgets every two minutes.

I think he thinks I'm a social worker.

But I know his mother's father was Maximo,

who owned most of Alameda,

and built the church and their little peach house,

and the dance hall which sparkled at night in the desert,

and which he, Ernesto, used to scrap at.

I tell him about my yellow house and my porch,

and he says he doesn't know

if he ever lived in New York. He lived in California,

and had a sister no one remembers because she died young.

Barbara, he says my mom's name.

The ink in the tattoo on his forearm has bled

much, into the skin around it. There, you can still make out

the curl of the E.

I lose against his three aces.

WE KNOW NOTHING, REALLY, OF DYING

The senses are a spasticity
of lies. We lift the remote control,
choose the tiniest spoon
for our chocolate pudding,
walk away from lovers.
We do not know when the ants
will come and devour everything.

He lost his left leg first,
numb after a night of fighting
with Mom.
We circled around his cane,
a gift from his friend Arnie.
We touched the fish carved into it;
a scene of pond life.

He said it felt like ants were swarming
his legs and nettling,
a million sticky feet taking him backward
into pupae stages.
He had always been a little clumsy
as I am now,
and I, too, wonder.

And then his right leg vanished.
His cane became defunct,
making way for the chair,
a technological clumsiness,
the gathered children always
doing the moving,
the pushing and carrying.

Once, I had begged my mother
for chocolate-covered ants.
They tasted like honey pots,
Mom made Jell-O instead,
one tiny bit
of stubborn gelatin—black cherry
boiled with horse bones.

It was at night when I heard him call.
Their beds were already separate.
His reading light was on,
the books were many layers
on the little side table
like cut leaves in a pile.

He had been short of breath,
was scared it was his diaphragm

failing.

That maybe the M.S.

had reached far enough inside

to pull the last of it away.

The ants driven even deeper,

their sugary

bodies in multitudes,

communicating a crustaceous desire,

tight shiny bodies manifested

in his core.

Moisture from the sliding-glass door

condensed; it fogged out our quiet talk:

his fascination with the cosmos.

His illness was never quick

like the assembly of an ant colony,

thousands of units parading

around the center,

parading

around the dead thing:

the skin of a frog,

the shell of a praying mantis,

it lingered like night hours

going by too slowly for a child

afraid of windows

filled with large crows.

In bed,

hours after he fell asleep,

the ants crawled up his arms,

all one hundred thousand

sterile sisters.

A congregation on the skin

above his heart.

REVELATO

Impossible
work, really.
Like placing
pebbles exactly
where they were
already. The
steadiness it
takes...and
to what end?
It's so easy
to forget again.
- Kay Ryan

O voi ch'avete li 'ntelletti sani,
mirate la dottrina che s'asconde
sotto 'l velame de li versi strani.
-Dante Aligieri

We have made it past the mountains to our home, and have

forgotten where that is.

God gives us monoliths to hide behind.

I asked God to help me remember.

God said,

Remember the old house on Sarah Lane?

Cherry tree leaves slicing your cheek as you ran past.

Remember how it had

Pebble picked up.

Pebbled marked with

brown-as-cocoa striations around its belly.

Pebble picked a hole in my—

Forgot

to place

the avocado tray

on the Formica kitchen table.

It's ugly; it gets me to remember

something.

                                        I can't articulate.

It's a problem with the myelin,

My dad says.

                        Somewhere it forgets to send the message.

It petrifies,

I say.

                                Stones thrown behind our heads,

                                            where they go,

                            what they find on the other side,

                                    are we made of this action?

In Quechua we have a name for that.

It's in my dreams almost,

almost a said thing

almost, almost.

Pebble picked up by the house in Alameda

shimmers and looks like what the brain must

grey and floating in liquids,

a closely watched flower

blossoms in the desert.

And then God said,

The mountain,

they all climb.

Repair him.

I said.

God said,

Hide.

They actually rolled the stones down.

The main street couldn't be completely destroyed

because it was carved out of the mountain.

Thoughts are full as copper buckets

filled with clear water.

The sentences have rippled far,

too many years of abandon;

the house demolished

by freeway.

Lift the wing of the bird
see the heart beating inside
the feathers marked
the little veil of the thumping, thump
the little strands of my grandfather's hair
wet with oil
the mind underneath, beating
the words he knows

Mire lo que he perdido
hermanito.
¿A dónde se fue?
¿A dónde fuimos hermanito?
Words at the bottom of an unfathomable

                                                          fog

Veil me.
Do not let me despair.
Please God, do not let me.
I see you turned to stone in Your mind.
Place your hands over my

                          hardness of heart, blindness, revelation,
                                bird heart, beating, beating, beat.

Outside by the trees, napkin trees.

A roadrunner.

A speckled roadrunner, red eyes.

Just stopped out by the trees. He had

what looked like a wreath of feathers

that made a fine white necklace around his collar,

and was described by my grandfather,

and retold and retold and retold.

The roadrunner stopped.

But my father said,

It's not a collar Ernesto, birds don't have those.

Roadrunner made the day stop,

a pebble lodged in his throat,

a pebble picked up from the ditch

smelled like water.

Drought in Alameda for four years.

Roadrunner stopped his throat

looking for a drink,

he got sand and small pebbles,

or one pebble, stuck.

Later, I dreamt

his stomach was torn open and there was a large neuron

in there,

like a hand, like a hand missing a hand.

Stopped,
Ernesto said.
Stopped like he was filled with rocks,
like the feathers concealed river stones.

Here is the *Corrido*:

The men swallow the stones
Looking for sustenance
Look too hard, men, you get stuck in your voice
Look too hard men, I turn you to stone.
Nebula is all mixed up in his hair.
Fine webs of crystalline-white gossamer.
The strands of jellyfish fibers and milkweed arms.
Tiny planets at the tips of hairs, blue planets,
planets with rings and moon shadows.

I tell my grandfather, Ernesto,
You have parts of the stray universe in your hair.

I used to be a barber,
he says.
Picked up a stone beneath a bridge,
lucky to be standing.
One, after a flood that turned red

because of clay deposits in the earth.
One by the ocean
when he was still a boy.
One found in a cracked bottle of brandy.
One, at the marriage of my mother and father,
in the courtyard
outside the Alameda church.

A fence.
It's all he remembers,
my grandfather,
not yet a man,
not yet with hair
white as paloma
feathers. A small wire
of a boy, all bone and teeth,
body of a scrapper
adopted to the Pereas;
they took him in and fed him.

His brother before he left,
I will come back to find you
as an old man.
his brother's face turned to the sun
and left, shadowed.

He held the bucket for the chickens
the shadow creeping over the earth
he kicked the shells of mud
and wished the drought would be over
wondered why his brother had left
at eleven years.
He followed his shape
until the dust and the horizon
made him dissolve.

Pebbles like comet pieces.
Pebbles like toadstools.

On the avocado couch I watch Ernesto sit
with the worry of morning,
fog eyes looking out,
looking past the filmy curtains
past them and into the yard of pebbles—
some ancient river bed.
He is pointing now
to the path outside.
Heart,
beating.
The dried up ditch,
the alfalfa field,

tremor of that boy,

tremor in his finger

like the dried shaft of yucca;

the wind catching it

just beyond the ditch.

HELENA

My grandmother's face
centered in a storm
watches a roadrunner from her window
the cigarette stapled
to her index and middle
She calls me
three thousand miles
You don't need a man to take care of you.
Her voice filled with weeds,
her voice, remember
the overwhelming river beneath the Sandias
open space before urban sprawl
the anger fixed in her eyes
the rumbling, *mujer*
from my grandfather's mouth
She wished to run
far into the llano
the sound of bees in her ears

How when she died,
she was found lodged between
the table and wall
standing despite her own death,

sentineled in the wake

of a great splitting

PATTERNS

For Kimberly

I was born in a crooked house in Alameda, New Mexico.
Across from a field of alfalfa. The alfalfa field was a tangled
lush expanse in a desert town. I was too young to go out into
it alone. My sister who was old enough would take us with
her. It was her world; it was her imaginary kingdom along
the sides of the ditch toward a house that was two-storied,
to the distant neighbor's house to play with sickly children.
With sticks, we would scrape up the mud and dirt into
patterns. We hardly paid attention to anything that wasn't
small. We collected the items necessary to create our
mudpies and our rock *ofrendas.* We repeat the same things
now that we are much older.

The line of familial
motherland
divided and shipped
and sent away
two hundred years
of our mothers
Nepumacena
Maria
Amelia
Apolonia

SPIRAL

Three spirals bound
to one another
Three sisters
at the edge of a stone
What is the cosmos but a radial movement outward?
To touch the fabric of one
to see the astral projection of the other
To forget for one moment
that it is only a projection

Spiral is not spire
Not arrows
Not shields
Not shells
It is a movement
the circles inside the corpus of a great tree
A slice of granite
A loop of river-bone
Our family of memory
The lost reflections of our arms and hands and our cheeks
and our eyes
the reflection at the edge of the mirror
The sound of a voice as it travels up from a basement

into the drawing room

absent of folk—absent of fire

a cold dream the dark earth has of clouds and air

The spire, the sword,

embrace all ways

to enter

touch the life force

touch that which only momentarily scrapes up

against

spiral that bleeds a shaft of light

as dust in a ray of sun floats in a doorway

MANUELA

For my great-grandmother and my sister
who told me the story of her death

Your coffin is open and it floats

along the current, breaking into splinters.

There are calla lilies in your hands,

and the blue flower dress you wear tears

at the hem;

your hair is yellowed and, like a web,

has come undone;

the tips are frayed,

they wave about in the black water.

It is as though your skin sinks deeply

into bones

exaggerating your skeleton

like a wax-paper flower.

Your rosary is in the river; the crushed

rose beads preserve

a thousand Hail Mary's;

they sink past my clutch.

The wide-mouth New Mexico sky is storming.

I enter the flood, feet covered in mud—

black with mossy fish

and long yellow leaves. Oh, I see you,

Manuela, and all of your life is swelling,

in the cottonwood coffin,

exploding like alfalfa in the fields.

I am screaming your name,

calling you like a lonely wolf

through the mountains,

afraid that without you I will starve,

become as empty as an ancient arroyo

by the Rio Grande.

So your name comes out

like a storm of hail from my throat

that flows like mercury

into your eyelids,

a dark stain forever

in the carved gully of your cheeks.

And gathering like many tiny raindrops,

I become one flood,

hiding the source deep in the caves

of those mountains.

Wading through the water, chairs,

and branches fluxing past me,

I can see your closed eyes, far off.

I imagine the way they used to look

before the flood,

before the cracked shells of dirt

of this desert held the water no more.

Before the mountains began to call you back home.

Before the river began to swell,

and the scent of rain made your hair spill

loose from those tight silver braids.

There is water in this dream, Manuela,

and it is part of us:

the river flood that swallowed Third Street,

feeding the parched red clay,

the adobe we make our homes from,

the old horno, and the ducks,

the cherry tree, and the wine bottles—

all of them, and you, Manuela,

floating away as I stand and wait for the sun.

THE DITCH

Uncle Albert left their chihuahua

in the Corrales ditch,

when he came upon her dead.

A little thing like that, and mostly blind,

she had wandered and followed the smell of water;

the tiny dog heard the water even if

the ditch had been dry for years.

But Albert, who had two girls at home waiting,

turned and walked away.

I remember that chihuahua sitting on my cousin's lap.

Turning her head to the side,

sniffing the thick smell of alfalfa.

Uncle Albert smoked a joint in the backyard,

and I saw hundreds of white sparks fall.

Later, a ditch filled with dead wood and leaves,

the dog lying on her side. My cousin sentinelled

over her like an overgrown thistle.

I REMEMBER THE DAY SWELTERED

burgundy button-back

the heat submerged sweat beading to the surface my mouth

after the long walking   past a heavy constant wish

      to cool us breeze us a dry gusting

from far in the dark grey out there

just sag, to pose—move to see   the gardenia flash

hand on hip cascaded citrus leaves woody shadow

             we must take this moment to be cool

THERE IS NO FENCE

There is no fence or, rather, there is this fence: a cloud of
linen napkins to separate the earth from sky. Call it the
gabled, white, cotton banner. It sets off in one direction and
is forever the line we should not cross. It is Sunday, a day for
hanging banners, a day for taking the silver percolator out.
Just you look at the work I have done. The walkway under a
canopy, the coffee in the Bermuda grass. Touch my bow,
later, when the edges begin to blur, feel the taffeta stiffness,
the creased warmth and wink of thread. This is proper fun,
the perfection in the creamer dish; this is the drinking
afternoon, this is our time.

CANTO I

Lend me your ear so that I may
decipher this.

Peach me, you fuck.

Pin-pricks even have codes.
What is the word for that squeak before a moan?

Somewhere out in the cosmos
we are all lit up.
We don't float,
We sparkle.

It's such a beautiful day, over there.

Eye on the pin-prick.
Like, the pin stays in there, instead.
We find that it has skin growing over it.

One hundred years the grandparents stayed together.
One hundred years on an avocado sofa.
Transfixed on making meaning.
He says, *Woman, I.*
He always says.

The night moon has a belt around it, or a noose.

They dangle.

Banana leaves spread about the floor,

slick and fragrant.

They drop.

She loved him more with his back turned.

She said she could hear him calling better.

How can we be there, when we are here?

Suspended in the air, while disconnected and lying on the

floor?

What is the best way to recall what has been lost?

He said, *Woman, I.*

She finally said,

I in-in you.

IN THE PHOTO OF FRIDA

She wears bougainvillea in her braids;
Smoking, lost some breath, and petting a deer.

After she died the room smelled of glass jars
filled with odorous leaves and wood smoke.
Some small children wondered at the extravagance
of her life, wondered at the *calacas* hanging about.

When the family left, Diego sliced a pear,
red as a cardinal, and put it between the sheets,

and at night, across time
I find that these walls chirp,
that the radiator is scratching in my ears;
the sounds of water moving through pipes in this house,

and the sounds of making love beneath the bed
only once or twice, but I swear they climaxed.
And the generations of women in my family whimpered;
I fell fast asleep each time,
the air, so dry and hot my hair stuck to the wall.

Desperate to find that photo,

I am busy forgetting quickly

I want to see the flowers—

if they are wilted at all;

if the photograph was in color;

if she is looking at me, or at Diego.

She had loved him and held that love

like death in the womb,

until it crusted at the edge of the photo.

No, Lover, I'm busy letting blood.

BROKEN GHAZAL OF FRIDA IN THE MIRROR

I want to be there in the room that opposes the mirror.
I want the room to be shades darker, claret.

Madrugada and the cream in your cheeks, Frida, a table
filled with citron, star fruits, and gardenia.

And I want to look in the mirror to see only myself now,
to see that the flies have all gone, not collected on your legs.

I want the intricate patterns on your dress, the animals
stitched,
so that they open their mouths for feeding.

Star fruit, and the waxy tablecloth. The Muscadelle grapes
painted on canvas, the flies on both sides of the mirror.

The animals now, with their starry, open eyes,
open with their threaded claws, open that wound of.

A closed black embroidery.
A monkey flared at the heart.

And our eyes open and hungry before us.
The reds wash over the linen.

DYAD

She wishes she had the ability to become larger.
The monolith is pointing her toward herself.
She hates that direction, better to wash a hand, walk
backward, turn away from yourself, eat the fragments.

Swallow a river of arrows pointed at each other.
This makes you bigger.
Too big you can't fit in your life.
Swallow a banner fluttering, pointed at home.

Small. She is fish eye, turtle egg.
The first map she makes is on the skin of a cloudy
mushroom. On it is written a correspondence:

the two selves looking on opposite sides
of a dividing line. Where my hand points, the other
is reflected. She is four now, she is an infinite tiny self.

ERES DEL POBRE SUR

Eres del pobre Sur, de donde viene mi alma:
en su cielo tu madre sigue lavando ropa
con mi madre. Por eso te escogi, compañera.
                    Pablo Neruda

You are from the poor south

the lace of beginnings

my mother her mother her mother

we share a common ancestry

we come from the place of mystery

should I call out your name

for the first time?

should I point you out in the crowd?

my mother says

don't lie to me

she says you and I are one

we wash the clothes together;

we always will

you are from the poor south

from the valley.

APPLE ORCHARD

Corrales, New Mexico, summer 1982

I.

We drove past the river and into Bernalillo.

There were crosses in my aunt's eyes.

The mountains call you back, she said.

The Sandias rose before us.

Clean pink peaks and the crags below—dark and greenish.

We drove into the dim patches.

Beyond the old house was the apple orchard.

San Juans and Roman Beauties were close to dropping.

We would be picking soon—culling and shining.

Wild asparagus grew in patches among the trees.

II.

She watched her mother being lowered into the ground.

A childhood wrapped in an old black dress.

She went crazy—all fury and open-mouthed

over the coffin.

My aunt held her back.

She made sounds like horses running.

My aunt's arms stretched out, gripping the coffin.

She struggled to climb on top.

I was too young; I sat in my mother's lap,

everyone watching everyone crying

and Uncle Benny falling to the floor.

Mama, Mama.

III.

Beyond the orchard, a ditch,

attractive with slender saltgrass and buffalo grass,

infested with piquant creosote

and in the bed, a roily nest of water.

Beyond that ditch, the earth stopped.

The edge of the world stayed back, beyond the ridge,

waiting.

My uncle said there were alfalfa fields that went on and on

until they hit the mountains.

But I knew what was really there.

I knew the smell of green apples the same way.

The familiar dreams of falling over that edge,

sun in my eyes, the taste of dirt,

the itchy tall grass and weeds, giving way.

I could smell the horses far off in the neighbor's field.

I could feel the void beneath my leather sandals.

IV.

My grandmother lost her face in the mountains.

She watched them the year she broke,

watched them turn gray, to pink, to red.

She saw things in them.

Once an Indian's face,

another time, her own

looking back.

EATING HEART

The fields of the valley go dark,
and there is violence in the summer rain,
a thudding as it hard-hits floor, splashes,
cuts into the vines.

Oh fish. Oh head of the scorpion.
He hands the gift to me; I eat it.

Sopping limb, body, fog,
center swaying into the mirrors,
a dazzling shadow in the mirrors,
blood in my eyes,
when I touch my face there is nothing.

The field takes me back:
blackened grapes bursting, clematis in the veins,
ferns uncoiling in the system's passages.
I swallow tips of left ventricle,
watch it drain like the valley,
like heart-shaped grape leaves petrifying,

sugar pulp rushing through arteries,
the familial blood lines rushing past,

an arroyo unraveling into a river,
a momentum of salty parts.

And us, now
you in me
you fed to me.

Black birds flying
close enough.
Feel their hanging bellies,

a fluttering like the fish hearts
the beating, beating
then dropping,

The sun sweats today
all this sacrifice,
iodine on my tongue
a memory of the sea.
Between the leather of vines,
the rodents in the irrigation tunnels.

Bring me back to three chambers,
the scuttle beneath the nerves

Heart eater. Exiled from orange trees;

under the great balanced day,

the heart beating an echo after its lifetime.

He carried it to me,

the branches of the heart;

they still suck, they drink.

Bring me back

into a cave of leaves,

looking for a window beyond the field,

a light in the window.

THE FLOODING IN EL LLANO

coming in to look I am in and out

this valley is in the flood plain

the moon sheds its water in the desert   cyclic

he was a carpenter   she a seamstress

looking into their house

a wooden chair against a carved chest

against a wooden chair

his gift to her

La Virgin de Guadalupe carved

into the pine-wood

then flash flood in *el llano*

they bobbed and knocked in the center of the street

as everything moved darkly away

~

el llano is close as a ghost story

the mothers lift themselves

each night

their gowns are sheets   legs slide over

head of grasses   they search for the desert plains

hands push through darkness

strum lace curtains until they hit the heavy wooden door

then they are outside

little brown feet shuffle

through silver and needle

grass

the yucca plant is a cloud of moths

lured from subterranean cocoons

their milky bodies vibrate inside waxy blooms

the mothers follow the road that has never been paved

into the dark plains & gathering

gathering

~

when the mothers leave

the fathers are asleep

the children in dreams

holding hand to hand to hand

running with the wind across their hair   a streak

lip and eye   they forget their bodies

a bed in the corner to catch a sliver of moon

the women shuffle into el llano

el tecolote flies hidden by clouds   tracking

~

before the valley knows it is morning

the bread bakers are kindling their hornos

like the call to prayer   but silent

el tecolote looks into windows

the children return

the women return

the men turn on their sides and open their slack mouths

the insects wake first   the bakers never went to sleep

~

el tecolote is the dream with wings

swimming between trees

reminding them

they will forget the dream

the mothers will not remember the un-paved road

with too much work to do

they tell stories of *el tecolote*

but will forget how they learned the stories

they will never know what the water knows

as it swallows the reflections of all things

ACKNOWLEDGEMENTS

Grateful acknowledgment is made to the editors of the following publications where these poems first appeared:

The Acentos Review: "Sarcophogi in Glass Houses"

Narrative Northeast: A Literary and Arts Magazine: "Spiral," "In the Photo of Frida," "Broken Ghazal of Frida in the Mirror" and "Velella Velella"

In the Grove, the special tribute issue, *Pakatelas:* "The Horno"

Riverlit: "The Discovery"

Silenced: Unheard Voices: "The Day Sweltered," and "There is No Fence"

Thanks to those at the Cornell University's Graduate English Department for choosing my poem, "Revelato," for the Robert Chasen Memorial Poetry Award and for the generous writing fellowship.

Also, thank you to Paul Genega, Pamela Hughes, Toni Mergentime Levi, Bill Hughes, and to everyone at *Three Mile Harbor Press* for believing in my work.

Special thanks to my mentors: Lee Herrick, Corrinne Clegg Hales, Kenneth A. McClane, Carmen Tafolla, Jean Janzen, Helena Maria Viramontes, the late Phyllis Janowitz, and also to the late Arnie Nixon.

Thank you to my friends for their support over the years and over the miles: Autumn Watts, Pelin Ariner, Sylvia Savala, Ire'ne Lara Silva, Dana Koster, Julie Brown, Lauren Alleyne, Dawn Lonsinger, Daniel Chacon, Kenneth Robert Chacon, Tim Z. Hernandez, David Campos, Michael Medrano, Devoya Mayo, Jon Hickey, Tien Tran, Stephanie Riden, and Randa Jarrar.

A huge thank-you to my amazing family—from the badlands of New Mexico to Fresno, California in a grey Toyota van: Mario L.M. Baca, Barbara Baca, Kimberly, Mario, Caroline, and Jason.

Thanks to all my uncles and aunts: John "Buck," Emily, Patricia, Richard, Ernest, Dolores, Rudy, Verna, Albert, and Julie. You were my childhood and the songs and stories you told were instrumental in my writing of this book.

Thank you to my grandparents, now gone from this world, whose lives inspired these poems: John and Helen Baca, Ernesto and Lillie Garcia.

Thank you to my nieces and nephews for being curious bright lights: Bryan, Devyn, Simon, Alexander, Amelie, Sarafina, and baby Emma.

Thank you to Erin Webster for the use of her artwork, which graces the cover.

And thank you to my husband, Curtis Messer, for your love and your music.

OTHER BOOKS BY THREE MILE HARBOR

Please visit us at: www.3milehaborpress.com